WHEN EVE WALKED

ALSO BY LINDA V. CULL

Where The Light Lives:
A True Story about Death, Grief and Transformation

WHEN EVE WALKED

POEMS BY
LINDA V. CULL

WILARA PRESS

First published 2020 by
WILARA PRESS
PO Box 360
Inglewood WA 6932
Australia
lindacull.com

© Linda V. Cull, 2020

This book is copyright. Apart from any fair dealing for the purpose of private study, research, criticism or review, as permitted under the Copyright Act, no part of this book may be reproduced by any process without written permission. Enquiries should be made to the publisher.

 A catalogue record for this work is available from the National Library of Australia

ISBN 9780994359322 (paperback)
ISBN 9780994359339 (ebook)

Printed in the United States of America
Cover and Internal Design by Damonza
Author Photo by Robert B. Cull

For Mary

Contents

1. Hidden

Red . 3
Breathless . 4
Shadows . 6
Solitaire . 7
Armitage . 8
Six . 10
Route to Hades . 12
Legends and Men . 14
Pennies . 21
Epilogue . 22
Avon Calling . 24
Time . 25
Seeker . 28
Every Woman . 30
Valentine . 33
Nightingale . 34
Beautiful . 36
Wharhola . 37
Abode . 38
Crumbs upon the Floor . 44
Hope . 46
Prayer . 48
Charcoal on Paper . 49
Final Hour . 52

2. Rising

Saffron Silk . 57
Eyes, Wide . 58
Before Dawn . 60
Blue . 61

Shedding Skin . 62
Ripe . 65
Spirit of the Land . 66
Now . 67
Tilted Moon . 68
Buttered Dreams . 70
Sestra . 72
The Word . 76
Temptress . 81
Incline . 82
Autumn Leaves . 84
Breathe . 86
End of August Nights . 87
Olive Tree . 90
Summer's Eve . 92
Queen of Dance . 93
After Dusk . 94
Venus . 95
Demeter . 96
Enchanted . 98

3. Risen

Ancestors . 103
Romp . 104
I Am Eve . 106
Madame Fire . 108
Beloved . 110
Fear . 112
Matilda Bay . 114
Song . 116
Breeze . 117
Wise, Old . 118
Green Grasses . 119
Oh, Life! . 122

What Dreams May Come . 124
Wedded Vow . 125
Golden Eyes . 128
Intimacy . 129
One Last Time . 130
To Love . 132
Being . 137
Rebirth . 138
Yallingup . 141
Augusta . 142
Homecoming . 144
Sun . 145

All the poems contained in this collection were written in my early twenties when I had many spiritually transformative experiences. It has been my direct-lived experience that creativity inspires a union with the ultimate power and is an effect of that union. Then, I was unfolding my womanhood. These poems, therefore, speak of the divine feminine; hidden, rising – then risen. *To Spirit, my thanks are due.*

L. V. C.

WHEN EVE WALKED

1.
HIDDEN

Red

The walls are chipped
and cheapened by the stale
colour of paint.

The room smells of cigarettes,
old decaying folk
and tobacco pipes.

The carpet is red,
the carpet is roaring red.
The room is half full.

I'm half empty.
The carpet is
red.

BREATHLESS

His foot by the door,
sliding back and forth along the floor,
thinking I was alone—
but I'm not,
my stomach in knots and butterfly wings
like dreams trapped inside of me.
Damp darkness – no air to breathe:
Who might you be?

Waiting for him to announce himself,
I gather my wits,
my scattered bits and p i e c e s
between dreams and waking.
I grip at a tight face,
rack my posture,
sit upright in a chair,
confront him with a piercing stare.

In an altered state of mind,
with altered senses as my defences,
ready to act in a second
if he reckons to come near me
in an attempt to poach me
or to encroach upon my will.
Then – I shall *rise*
like a lioness!

From a state of half sleep
to the balls of my feet,

ferociously – if need be,
I will scream and shake the house
awake! If he should dare
take from me
what is not
for his taking.

Shadows

Tortured is my silence.
Solemn is my gait over grasses at dawn.
Solemn fellows beneath my toes

trample the cooling shadows.
Gardens in their shallow slumber,
are startled by my wonder.

What make they of my questioning tongue?
My loose words,
rebounding words.

Solitaire

My belly is full.
My throat heaves
with unsung songs,
stagnant tears,
great expectations,
loneliness.

When one becomes
aware   she is alone:
born alone, die alone,
hold to conversations
with God
alone.

Tired days, shut lids,
climbing through the
night sky to collect
my solitary p i e c e s ,
to have them meet
after all this   time.

Armitage

Men walk the street on
Armitage.
Eyes – run tracks.
Sounds – echo in drains.
Cars – obscure lanes.
He sleeps. He thinks
and waits,
and waits,
he waits. He waits,
unravelled and reluctant,
wanting to deceive me,
wanting a more beautiful life than this.

Yet, beauty adorns him.
He throws it   away.
Still, he waits,   he waits,
fingers combing through his hair,
he elongates his transient stare,
walks the street on
Armitage
down
in the out of town,
where people live on stale air
and dirty fingers comb
dirty hair.

My breasts beckon a fruitful truth.
No truth – but every way.
If only he knew which way was up,

he would depart the ground for the sky,
dance upon heaven's eye—
if a dog had the answer lying on a worn couch,
a dog he would want to be,
but a dog is more loyal than he,
and so, he considers himself—
he considers himself
waiting like a dog
he never wanted to be.

Six

I touch my face – skin – oiled.
Sticks to a tiled wall,
I wait for the six train.

We wait together
beneath the ground like moles,
startled by fluorescent lights,
sobered by the breathless air that is
still, and heavy, and still.

The seconds have slowed.
Eyes – move along tracks—
towards faces, along backs.

Air so still, and baited, and battered
upon my brow.
I might climb the tiled wall—
smells of a tired day.
Sweats   pants.

Wipe my face with a tissue—
the back of my hand.
So still   the scene.

So still the scene. In the heat
relief – runs – my heart,
a breeze – runs – the tracks
on the arrival of six.
Six on the green in a city that never waits.

Hurrying for tomorrow – an air-conditioned carriage.
Toes and shoes. No one cares if I sit or stand.
No one cares from where I come   to where I go.

I have never cared more for shoes and feet
and painted toes, than those
upon the floor of number six.
We are strangers in the great city, yet
our swollen feet share the heat   out east.

Route to Hades

Do you see youth marching by?
With eyes to the sky,

shoulders hung on shame,
knowing this is not a game.

In   stride   another   mile,
doom strapped to a shallow smile.

Take your place at the gate.
Hurry – before it's too late!

With my foot on the edge,
careful – don't tilt the ledge.

Knocking on the Footman's door,
I'm startled by mother's call.

She comes to comb my hair
to the tune of despair

and begs the breath of death
to renounce its glare.

But in the sight of guns,
she abandons her little one.

Sorrows in the wind wail their names
as folk hear voices in the rain.

They pray aloud to muffle sins.
Rancid tears   leap   from   their   chins.

Take an ear to the sky.
You can hear all the lies

from men in suits
who reside in disguise,

whilst those who are spared,
live to mourn these affairs.

In time oceans cleanse the shore.
Thus, the sands are stained no more,

and the one who forgets
is devoid of all regret.

Peel back the skin of men
and you will see the blood of them.

Legends and Men

1
Disturbed.
Afraid.
Betrayed.
Reluctant to go, to stay
by you and me and men
on a steaming day
hot enough to choke life,
to resurrect the woman.

Instead, I walk the street
and blistered feet
and blistered wanting:
to climb, to reach, to shout out and turnabout,
to see man as man, unlike me.
And I – a gem beneath a rock,
beneath the dirt of earth and smoke
to choke me on a day too hot to eat, to sleep,
to reach the tops of men.

By his seat I sit with blistered feet,
eyes to see between his legs,
intrigued to see him in the heat,
too close to breathe on.

2
Of men and smaller than men,
he holds himself by the beard of other men,
comes for me and stands,
steps
down from men
into my sights,
bends his head and stupors.

In every perfect moment,
a poet sings and loves the scene.
Sits upon my bed.
Guitar and casual strings
to stitch and mend
the broken moulds of modern men.

I love his moment,
she loves the moment.

The chatter belches his head and stupors,
stones falling from the ceiling
bust the heads of wretched men.
Comes for me and stands,
steps
down from men
into my sights.
I avert the smaller than men.

3
Close I float
through the glass eye
into night sky.
Beer and white wine,
chairs whine for a taste of social slaughter.
Speak badly of friends.
The men they shatter
and scatter themselves between lies.
I fall to dive into the cries of shattered eyes.
Hearts of glass that cannot bend
around his concrete feet,
and my swollen knees,
and his watered down belly
into a caged chest—
his stiff arms and neck and hollow legs.

Up into thoughts of strong men I climb,
over the boys of old worn school days.
Sit and lie, and negotiate a way
away from my bubbled thighs.
They laugh as I watch them.
I yearn for truer friends
than boys who consider themselves
the life of empty men.

The boys of shallow souls – *scold her.*
I look away and – *hold her*
from the reach of young boys who cannot – *know her*
past the smoke and drunk rings
to count the days upon my
peridot fingers.

4
I rejoice myself, my heart, my breasts.
Drink coffee with sugar and stir and spread my legs
apart—
a man pauses—
passes me a magazine and I accept   smile—
cannot talk with biscuit before my breath.
I go to speak – he says – smile again.
I think of him
and slowly turn the pages, over again
in my head   to read
of my passionate desire
to consider when
air and fire
will sweep the earth
of all the liars.

5
I see Jesus.
Stand   my tiptoes on Adam
looking lost in heaven.
I wait and strain myself
to see his face   his long brown hair.
My short brown hair frames his burden.
Across his shoulder frame
my thoughts bleed,
his waist bleeds,
and from between my legs, the night begins to
scream
aloud!
Into the street he is silent,
begs and sweats
against an urban dwelling.
Broke.
The youth are smelling of a dying breed,
an urban swelling
draped in white cloth.
Needs an art, the full-moon to believe in.

I bleed to understand him
and I die to know him
to complete my own equation.
Standing on a smoke butt cement throne.
And misconceived. And misconstrued.
Still I wait alone – we wait together.
Old hags shopping together,
looking through the distance,
clutching our fast-food plastic bags.

6
The morning brewed a coffee-coated woman,
richly scented
in a stale sleep,
my stale defeat fermented.
Nothing too new to awaken me to.
Arise by my new defences
as he washes his face and combs his hair.
I present myself somewhat differently from the night.
Into day I smell his breath that once enticed me.
I cup my face and cradle my bosom.
Before noon breaks dawn with a sombre mood,
a sombre groove
into my face with a silver spoon,
he stirs my empty cup,
sugar lumps stick as I walk on the linoleum floor
and I regret that he should so easily forget me.

7
My pregnant belly – Infinity's child.
Bear my destiny into the hands of an old woman,
senile and anonymous,
crooked hips, her sunken lips,
her bones grate upon the gravel,
her walking stick as she hobbles,
her elastic bosom wobbles.
Deflated – points towards the sun.
My child comes from an iridescent white-glitter moon,
rose enamel cheeks and golden eyes.

How sad to walk the street
in shoes afraid to speak
to all the people passing by
with words upon the e n d o f t o n g u e
and touch upon   the end   of tips.

PENNIES

A dirty train floor
holds the knees of a man
begging for pennies.

I watch him,
I watch people watching him,
I watch myself   look away.

He begs and is not shy to beg,
he begs for pennies,
he cries for pennies,

he sings a sweet melody for pennies.
He holds out a white paper bag
with his dirty hand.

His is the voice of destitution.
These are sounds the moderate resent to hear.
A woman holds a child in her arms.

Her eyes are not shy to jeer him.
A man begging for her unwanted pennies
is the rock upon which my head lies.

Epilogue

Entrenched beneath the house are his feet.
There he rests, and from there he reaches for me.
A solid frame we built around his head
with wide hallways and high ceilings.
I like the high ceilings.
I can climb and still, my head is free from the fist
but not from the fall.

Onto the porch—
this is the nicest port I have *ever* tasted.
Our hands lift our faces
with another sip from the thumb.
Sentimental talk and intimate exchanges.
Bravado
in the shallows of a wooden barrel.

We descend from our predecessors, somewhat awkwardly.
We decline to behave as we suppose we ought to.
And yet, we do something of what we ought to.
Somewhat awkwardly – *vanity*
absent in some, gathers gladly around others.
Some are shy, I admit, some *are* shy.
Though, they appear arrogant, at best.

Discreet shyness. Come again. Come again.
Friend, pal, potential husband – *my God!*
How the mind challenges everyone,
r u n s way before the   step
Like a resounding roar before the cat:

"Tinkerbell, here, Tinkerbell…"
yes, yes, yes… pet, pat, pat.

To say then, he was born bold   echoes.
He now lies barren in a box
whilst she, as ever, is bedraggled
and in desperate need of his attention.
Forgive us for our ignorance and intolerance.
Excessive   borrowed.
How grossly alike we are, in fact, bookends.

Tomorrow we flick through albums,
fingering pictures of the dead.
Very predictable – better, still
we smell his clothes.
Think the stink smells pretty.
Let go. Let go bedraggled widow
and imagine   *you were always alone.*

Avon Calling

I waited and waited
until four-o'clock
in the morning.
Avon called.
I bought makeup
but, no God—
I scribbled my failings
in red lipstick
across the ceiling
so, when I'm dead,
my eyelids rolled back
in my head,
I may recall
how I went wrong.

I cried and cried
into an empty bowl
that tipped over
and wet the mat
with somethingness
that smelt sour.
I screamed for an hour
but still, no one came.
Perhaps,
they haven't received
my silent screams
in the mail.
I posted ten letters,
ten days ago.

TIME

Why do my eyes cry, and my insides,
they weep?
My heart is too sad to speak,
curled round like a rusted coil
in a hard leather seat
as a babe in a temporary crib.
Silently, the room is falling asleep
with discarded memories at my feet
like the words of those who have come here to sit.
They sat, to chat,   to *chitter-chatter*.

But no more, what a bore.
Not a sound, not a breath.
No heart that pounds inside my chest.
My feet, my hands, are nowhere to be found.
My head is lost beneath the ground,
a yawn as tired as my closing eyes
in flutter with my jagged thoughts
and images in disarray.
My dreams at the ends of carpet threads
in weaves of shaded colours.

Smell of charred tobacco leaves,
the stale pages of books
with their stories shut
of lies and tales of drunken truths
that spilt a pack of playing cards
in muted melody, as the piano stands
in its sullen wake

and the paintings shake.
The ceiling fan cuts away the walls
in scattered shadows.

A sleep so deep I may drown
in my dreams that peel
the skins to my soul,
and this to be told:

>Beautiful me,
>where have you been?

>*Wandering the earth*
>*in search of my dance.*

>Beautiful me,
>where have you shone?

>*Light of the moon,*
>*I turn to the sun.*

>Mystery me,
>where do you go?

>*Footsteps in sand*
>*to bury the yester.*

>Beautiful me,
>where do you stand?

In piles of salt,
she rests in my hand.

Beautiful me,
when to return?

Cometh the winds
I ride on tomorrow.

Seeker

I have travelled far and wide
despite my tired feet,
kicked up sand with my bloodied toes,
gathered the sky between my hands
and placed it in a jar on a shelf.

I have slept with my fingers crossed
beneath my pillow and dreamt
of my secret wishes   coming true.
I have scrapped my knees along the road
thinking the answers lay between the stones.

I have even jumped from the branches
of a tall tree and flown   for seconds
before my heels stomped the grasses
down. But, no, it was not enough.
Don't tell me otherwise.

There is nothing else for me to do.
Nothing that I, or you,
can think to convince me of.
I have spoken to people who hear,
I have spoken to animals that hear.

Yesterday, I saw flowers on a hillside, in bloom.
I bent down to see if they had ears too—
they had ears, but they didn't hear me.
I spoke to the birds, I sang.
They were afraid, I ran.

I looked up at the sun and lost my sight.
I heard the ocean roar along the shore
but then it rolled away   forever.
I thought:
'Tis not enough for a dying heart.

Every Woman

Enough thought of what may be – or not be.
Think not the night away in an awkward dream.
Take time into your hands with urgency and sculpt it
as you please,
but do not sit in contemplation
of that which has yet to be.
Go on to live that which you have not yet seen.
Take yourself into action before the next hour passes.

And for a shower I go,
undressing of my sleeping clothes
in stale dress from a stale night ago,
removing my bra
and my breasts hang free,
and the air embraces—
my legs – between.

In length of mirror,
I look at myself over and from below
imagining what he has seen of me on show.
My fingers touch my flesh to feel what he has felt.
I put a finger up close to my nose softly, so soft,
my skin which his tongue has tasted and preened.

Had he not touched me from head to toe
and touched me deep below,
I would not have felt in places where
I had never before felt myself go.

I reach to touch my breasts in sight of this,
taste my salted hand,
bite my skin with tease,
lick my shoulder wet
to feel this wet against my cheek.

I am woman – *all woman*.
And for this moment, I am every woman,
with every piece of me in harmony
in feel of the smoothness of myself…
my body in form; curves and rolls as fruit in swirls,
ripened and ready to pick and devour—
succulent, delicate, and dripping delicious.

Suddenly, I stammer a sigh in voice of my lie,
for so often I feel nothing of the woman inside—
to be a woman, not of body but of mind – *a dream*.

Rather, I be the famished fem of the teething kind,
and in bad dreams, the droves of men may come and go
yet, still, my heart be lone
in wish of nothing more than myself as whole
and to be not a beggar or thief anymore.

Drenched by naked thoughts such as these,
I turn the rain upon my head to appease my senses—
warm and wet, the sweats of the steaming shower
clear the clouded hour.

Out of the shower and into fresh clothes,
I costume in tones of night—

in satin and lace underwear   I step.
My dress fans about my shaven legs,
hair of sweet vanilla scent dried to its very end,
dance upon my shoulders bared.

I am a vision of beauty,
though neither a simple vision
nor a simple beauty am I.

Immaculate and admired—
admire me in passing,
and I will consider myself, imperfectly,
yet, I know myself to be the perfect pose
with features so unlikely and of womanly pulp.
How do I not stir a man?

Having spoken not a sentence of story with me,
one is bound to the core of my intrigue.
So, gather ye quickly by my side—
and I will wonder   *why*.

VALENTINE

He has forgotten my face…

as day forgets darkened streets enmeshed with legs
and underwear beneath sparkling dress.
Stars behind eyes of drunken smiles and bated breaths;

where do the women go who stand and wait in shadows?
Lips lit by fluorescent masquerades
heavy under urban chains and nail polish chips—

I run away like a stale nose
turned suddenly from itself;
he has forgotten my face…

though his sight is a path of lace
stretched between posts of firing trees
that trumpet and gather together.

NIGHTINGALE

Gothic nightingale, haunted friend.
Conspiracy, claustrophobia, clairvoyance
and red candles,
checked tablecloth,
salted bread – along a suburban street.
Linear houses, cloned cars,
narrow footpaths.
People chatter,
strangers sit side by side.
Eyes – and Italian aroma.
Integration,
indulgent friend.
The underworld alights
by flirtatious intimacies.
Awkward day
unravels in a flurry.
Intimidations.
Eager – are you
to feel a sin
between your palms,
to feel the real night.
You confess—
oh, transient friend!
We run by wheels in the city,
glitter music, wind, wild feelings.
We sing
past luminous palm trees,
jaded street dwellers,
garnished extroverts.

(We care for none of them.)
We endeavour to be without care.
Freedom seekers.
We name the wind
that parts our hair.
Erotic postures – by public toilet blocks.
Back street light bulbs
sporadically
f l a s h
red
upon his navel.
A cigarette in the bushes.
Slowly, mindfully
manoeuvres his pelvis.
Thrusts the night – a ravaging sparrow,
turned on by the early show.
I'm at the edge
of his mysterious exchange,
crusted delight and rampant imaginings.
Intently—
I see into the illumination
by city lights.
A crisp autumn night.
My curves lie undefined.
Stars – the three quarter moon.
Acknowledge their hidden pleasures
that swoon
as men
attend only
to men.

Beautiful

Far more interesting are the interesting—
even more, the ugly interesting
than the beautiful dull,
for beauty will dull
and the dull beautiful,
dull those more beautiful;
the beautiful are together, beautiful.
The dull, together, dull.
Beauty too may be interesting.
The interesting – beautiful.
Worst of all, the ugly uninteresting,
yet, even they, are interesting to me.

WHARHOLA

I want to be a star, a *Wharhola!*
Created merely through speculation – *b r a v e* .
I want starlet eyes, red raucous lips
and lashes that lash out!

The crowds will *sigh*.

I want to live in a kaleidoscope sphere,
wear a chameleon's attire.
Starlet moments and pauses,
deep contemplative poses
amidst revelry and audacious vanity,
juxtaposed by pop and art.

Cities – with countless turns and reflections,
bellowing smoke from a can-can's hand.

Cool men are hot beneath blinking street lights.
Refined, adjusting their ties, the rain begins to fall.
Steaming postures – shadows jerk on walls,
when pretty suddenly steps out in her temptress heels:
a brunette – perfect eyebrows arch her perfect face.

She is gorgeous on the flickering screen.
He, so arduously arranges bated exchanges
in a silent movie that moves all too rapidly.

ABODE

1
The table is laid in a hurry, in a flurry:
olives, berries, radishes in clay bowls
moulded by the hands of a man. A woman. A *wow* man.
See the dirty fingertips – old.
In trail. In print. Fingerprints in the tint.

Boiled eggs in shells.
Me – Eve. (A young woman of delicate feathers.)
Preened. Ready to eat with clean fingertips.
Crack open a shell,
peel back a shell – in thought.

Smell – an unborn chick.
Jelly yoke sticks in my throat,
in half. A mother hen in half – I may *baff*
to the sound of a bell ringing in my head—
ring-a-ding-dong. Bong. Is it wrong to eat an egg?

Cracks my heart in half. A p a r t .
Rather, think not of the dead. *Quick!* Change my mind.
Turn my thoughts inside out. Shout. Out. *Enough!*
Sit on me if you must. Convince me—
no half babe has died for my merry dinnertime.

2
Incubation. Incineration.
Let me dine in peace, divinely.
In rhyme and harmony
meeting with mouths, in chitter-chatter, *splatter!*
Do you hear? Stop gnawing at my ear.

Cheeses of cows graze in meadows beneath the sun.
Packed together, one on one—
two and three. A hundred at once.
In a bunch, like dying flowers.
Tightly. In the heat. On a baking tray.

May I have some fresh bread
warmed on the fired coals?
Please – so I may ease my heart
and start over again—
I'm only human, from which the humane sprout.

Out of my head. Instead
I bathe in scents so sweet. Again, I heave.
Is it time to eat? No. *How unfair!*
I see my own inverted stare. A glare—
lurking out the moles from holes, beneath the earth.

3

Hear them knocking at the door: *knock knack*.
I turn my back. They shall be ignored.
A lack of charity. A moment of unprecedented clarity.
There be more for me — for me to eat. As in a treat
stewing. Meat crying in a clay pot.

Rotting in a belching pot. Burns on my skin, so hot.
I will treat myself to a fleshy feast — as could, would
a beast rising in the east. Falling from day.
Has come to sit on my hungry seat. *Still, hungry*.
Sitting on my seat with thoughts that eat at me.

Fill up on happiness by eating bread alone.
May I? Can I? *Greedily. Needily. Hungrily*.
Be satisfied on bread alone.
Does the silence condone my roasting thoughts?
In the oven. A misfit. I roast,

distracted only by my fantasy, as he dances with me—
Eve and he. Hand in hand. A man
with his oven mitts on. Who is he? *Answer me*.
Eager fingers pull apart that which tired fingers kneaded
but, I know not his name.

4
Tortured are my games in mind, never kindly.
Who is to know but me – of he – my fated lover, he.
Inflated. Debated. In doubt. Perhaps he will never be.
I breathe in another thought. Caught.
Somewhere between cracks and webs—

spiders whisper in the hall
about the faint knocking at the door
sounding something like before.
Though now, drowned, by the sound
of tongues dropping to the floor.

Flavours licking at my face like a kitten.
A hearty stew cooking on the stove – its paws up my nose.
Furring. Purring. Curling up my toes.
Reap! Reap! The silence speaks:
"Use your hands and feet to eat, if you dare."

In pair. Ten fingers a piece. Five on each. Ten toes.
Nobody needs to know I eat like an ape.
Twenty in sum. All to one. Sixty to everyone.
Between the three. Me, he and three. Gape.
Eyes like grapes. Plenty of teeth to smile like a crocodile.

5
Eyes sneak in spaces between faces at the dinner table.
Eyes able to rock the table top. *Stop the clock!* In time.
A shrine unto my undivided eye. One-eyed
as eyes eat before fingers can take or tongues can taste.
I cannot wait for another bite of my lip—

where is the dip and carrot sticks? I lick my lips.
Still face. The girl has grace.
Though, hunger, in cages, itches from behind my face.
Fish's scales scratching against my skin.
I rub my chin with flaking fingernails.

My stomach rumbles. *Rumble jumble.*
In a jungle of desires that never tires.
I stumble over my act—
his wife speaks of the heat above the broth
that stirs a wooden spoon.

Disgruntled. What? More. I hate to wait!
Let's begin to eat. He sharpens his teeth on his claws—
poking at me through the floor,
more eager to dine than I.
Could it be – I'm not hungry, after all?

6
Watching him eat at the corners of my sleep—
teething on his favoured talk,
drinking wine from clay cups.
Blood of grapes bleeds sorrows of great-hearted dreams,
yet to come, someday, in some distance away.

Amend. Amend. A bleeding heart!
Thoughts of darting animals, crying as they run. *Run away.*
Yum. Yum. Sin. Sin. Eat more than you can.
What a *scream* – rejoice.
Take plenty in your hands to eat.

Roll like a ball. Run like a bull.
Rise into the sky as the moon
and block out the night with rounded faces.
In the day, explode – into far off places, as the sun
with our bellies growing in the light, fills the empty places.

Delighted. In flight. His happy chatter races.
Then a bang – a clang! His clay fingers in dishes – *gladly*.
Eats of many wishes, as he so desires
to run with the shadows that sin in the hall.
There is knocking at the door.

CRUMBS UPON THE FLOOR

An audience awaits with bated breath.
A soft light turned upon the porch,
chimes relax the afternoon.
I feel teased and tested, I feel rather tempted.

His golden locks swept by the rugged winds.
Show his lovely face and eyes – offshore blue.
Life reflects beauty in he.
Glorious stranger who endears his spirit to me.

Forget you not my companion in mind,
with those ageless eyes in an infinite stare.
My silent words have kept these memories of mine
in hope our paths will cross in time.

From where do my secret pleasures come?
Seeped through pores in cotton boxes,
I presumed, locked away and hidden beneath a stairway.
Best not dream of man who lives for another woman.

And not of my gentle caress, yet
he inspires in me, a yearning for tenderness
as would my soul-sketched destiny
reaching forth from the ashes.

Save me these droplets of favoured thoughts,
in perspiration beneath my woollen coat.
Perhaps, he has forgotten her and comes instead for me?
Deeply, I am assured, we shall never touch as lovers do.

He drinks tea at my casual table
in search of casual counsel.
Strides his eyes by the withered garden.
It is raining heavily and my vision is impaired.

Excuse my greedy fingers and crumbs upon the floor—
if we eat, then we do not need to speak   except
my plate is quite   empty,
and in   silence,

my pant appears somewhat
d i t h e r i n g
and then
        distracting.

HOPE

Dream…
that I will come to know of love,
to feel it running my body in beads of blood.
What is it to love?
To know your thoughts in heart:
of body, mind, spirit, from the very start.
As the world unites – the universe to hold,
even, the stilling of the falling sun.
Having failed in love, today
and losing my way, again—
to live for love,
to draw breath for love,
wail and scream for love.
Still, it fails to come.
Life in corners of saddened souls.
It must be—
my absent delight,
for no longer without can I be.
I beg. I plead.
The day ahead is tomorrow – in line
with sights of beauty and shadowed sorrows.
Rolls of ocean floor,
deafens the yearner's call.
Having loved in a lifetime before,
it has been, I have seen eyes of the one.
To know the void,
to do without,
to behold – having lost once more,
departed the beloved.

With eyes in shade of suns,
and talk of muted tongues,
a handless touch, perhaps,
in hope of love.

Prayer

Oh, dear God – why hide from me?
In all desperation, I call out to Thee.
Be my companion in these lonesome hours.
Comfort my soul with song to end Your silence.

Oh, child of mine, waste not your breath,
'Tis in your eyes that My image does rest.
Wipe clear those tears which stain your vision
and empty your ears of sorrowful sounds.

For in the peace of one's boundless mind,
an echo you will hear, of the prayers uttered.
And while you ask of Me to be true,
know, that I whisper, these words back to you.

Charcoal on Paper

On this day, I have come upon a new sight, unseen.
Perhaps, I have been blind – as before.
My eyes closed. My mind drowned. I say
I see the sun overshadowed by its own hand,
squinting in the light – too bright.
This sight, I perceive in the dark of a splintered heart
of which dreams have blistered like blunders of past.
Yes. I have said before—
I would not be as I was then, yet
I am unchanged.
Nor have I broken away
but broken apart in thought. In heart.
Love,
loveless.

I would never have hoped this—
to be my question to an unknown one,
but I am rather tired of speaking alone unto myself.
Thus, I imagine a friend in you:
What is life?
I thought it was love.
Love is life but what is love?
I feel it only as a hunger that never feeds me.
It makes of me a beggar—
a criminal,
a liar,
an actor,
a child,
knowing not where it has come from,

knowing not where it pulls me towards.
Enticing me. Hounding me. Insanely,
for it goes by many guises,
roaming undetected.
When I hold it down, it rises to reveal me.
When I ride upon its back, it turns over to drown me
in sorrows that rape my soul, at depth
running
deep.

So, who am I, but a mortal to that which is immortal?
And who can I be but an all-ignorant being?
By the all-knowing one that alludes me—
desperately,
I am humbled by such mysteries,
humbled by my own imagination
that ceaselessly builds upon my broken bones
with dreams like palaces
that soar to heights above me,
rooted upon my decaying soils.
And though the winds of some distant destiny
tumble me down,
it goes again
with my chin ploughing the earth
in search of seeds to grow.
In hope, bruised though I am,
laid sprawled indecently before a fearful
fearsome world…
ever fearful of itself—
myself
alone.

We wish, before death,
to be known unto ourselves.
At least, unto each other.
To know what love truly is,
to live, and to be loved.
Beyond lust and desire and hope and dreams,
having loved *deliberately*.
Playing not in shadows below gravel ground,
as do the pitiful and passionless who make life from stone.
We pray in the dark, in whispers like burrowing ferals.
For others to know not who we are.
To not know we are as they – in pain – in joy.

Tomorrow we shall expire,
tomorrow we shall die
and become air that fuels the fire.
Together our souls will burn in flame,
returned, so we may being again
in hidden memory – but unforgotten
by the breath of love that shakes us now
to turn us inside out – before the end.
A kiss before the dead to rise again.
New dreams still warm as lips pressed on lips.
Love will shake us then.

Final Hour

I will take more
of the things I like.
I promise
a little bit
on the tip of my tongue—
no more than a crumb
and a swipe of butter—
not even a swipe…
less than a swipe,
half a swipe.
Tastes better with butter.

They mutter: "Reduced fat butter."
Reduced by a cow sliced in half
stuck with needles in its neck.
Thick and tasty…
oh, how very tasty!
One more mouth for good luck.
A good life: "Yes. *No.* Yes. *No.*"
I eat. *I seep.* I eat. *I seep.*
I cannot be sure
if I'm full and fat…
dare I devour the final hour?

2.
Rising

Saffron Silk

I close my eyes,
awakens the dreamer,
the hype   *the screamer!*
Wings of night
flap about my head,
pulse of a dragonfly
shivers inside my mind.
Ladies draped in saffron silk
flicking their goodbyes.
Bare the skin of perfume scents.
A thousand cents for every pose,
a powder for every nose.
Men in borrowed clothes,
voices robed in different tones.
Some are pretty. Some are proud.
Words of this. Words of that.
That, this, a *kiss*—
heels sound the polished floor,
opening and closing of the door.
A laugh in every glass with friends.
Waiters, wait, until the end.
A shiver runs up my spine,
a river runs through my mind;
a trickle,
a drip,
a dro p
of sweat…
I open my eyes.

Eyes, Wide

Open my eyes   wide.
A numb tongue   dumb.
No words to speak
but, to think.
A body on fire in bed.
Red sheets sweat,
kicked back in the night.
In flight   now
tangled around my legs,
toes pointed at the fan.
Clicks   clacks.
Turns the room about my head.
Moving the heated air
of no relief at all.
If only it could be cool   cooler,
for who can bare to sleep
in such heat?
Or to move, or stay
or blow upon my skin   wet.
Tasting of salt in beads,
running down the nape of my neck.
Stiff – from stuffed pillows,
foamed and feathered,
full of dust.
I rise.
I will not
fall
again
in bed

on folded
knees.
I see through
the window shades
upon the vivid
colours
of yet
another day.

Before Dawn

The sky is dirty at the horizon:
shady. Shaded in. Smeared.
Above that, it appears somewhat lighter,
and then darker once more.
It is early in the morn, before dawn.
I see two stars;
someone has forgotten to pack them away.
The haze reaches out.
There is blueness to the sky.

BLUE

The ocean, as we wade within its waters,
toes sunken in beach sands.
The sky wrapped around our minds,
like old silken gypsy rags.
Blue – moving the face of every life.
A new expression. A new day,
perhaps, even, a new way.
See, how all things come out to greet blue—
me, you, people – not seen before.
They come out from behind trees, standing tall,
casting shadows – bowing to the floor,
in sacred contemplation.
Flowers, eager, open their hands in friendship.
As peace comes to pass through scented fingers,
new colours are born. New costumes are worn.
Diverse. Uninhibited verse.
How sweet it is to smile like a flower.

Shedding Skin

I'm shedding skin and lizards cross my path;
little lizards, rustling dried leaves
and fallen bark.

Birth was a horrendous experience;
I was in so much pain!
Tomorrow—
it will be forgotten.

Father cut the shrubs shallow.
He pulled out our beloved lavender bush.
My sister cried.

He cut his thumb
and blood trickled
all over the pavement.
Everywhere, he went.
A splash of blood
later removed with water.

I was painting red spots on a canvas
anticipating this month's blood
to rush out of me.
My breasts, swollen and bruised.

What a horrendous birth it was—
painful.
Really painful and bloodied.
And doctor rooms:

doctors, nurses, hospitals – and dramas.
Great   big   dramas.

I'm tired of dramas
and suffering
and doctors.

Home is a marvellous place.
I didn't leave reluctantly.
I strode out the door, purposefully,
knowing life would take a second of my time.

But life lingers on.
It's a preoccupation of sorts.
Sometimes sweet,
sometimes sour,
and nothing is as it seems.

The day my father wounded himself,
I was wearing red knickers.
His blood,
my lace under garb,
all the same colour;
the same depth of colour.

I'm shedding skin.
I see broken shrubs as I walk by the river,
broken by dark cockatoos
that come before the rain
and shriek awful like wickedness.
I'd hide my head and pray,
howling inside myself.

Now, I don't even bend a tiny shadow.
I look at the birds—
how beautiful they appear
in the afternoon sunlight,
flying in the unhindered sky.

This morning, I began to bleed.
I talk of fertility with a woman friend.
I've come to anticipate another birth.
This is the pain.

My breasts expand out
and, into my bra,
my flesh rolls.
My stomach turns.

Ripe

Juices of pomegranates,
toffee of dates,
taste of figs
ripened with sensual syrup.

Blood red – pulsating with plenty.
I eat of every thought, *ravishingly*.
My flesh cannot bulge on thoughts alone.
I think.

Spirit of the Land

In meditating on countless trunks of trees,
I'd been seeking all kinds of features
where they ought not to be.
My mind was with feral sorts in bushes,
their eyes marked in bark
whilst wild grasses spat abuses.
I came to pass on by their perches,
a vision of yet another mirage emerges.
Eyes of tricks saw snakes turn to sticks.
Be it the magic of Moses before me
or be it that I am a fool,   but
I could have sworn to have seen
tribesmen fleeting alongside my car
in memory of their sun-browned faces.
An ancient spear, chiselling at my right ear.

Now

I remember hearing
someone,
somewhere
say before
that now only matters,
and so,
now is who I call forth.
Thus, for now, I'm glad
to be leaving the city lights
and empty delights,
to be leaving memories
that fester beneath
my vanilla-scented skin
like the rash
that has me itching
at my watch
with cold fingers
on a hot day
as I drive away.

Tilted Moon

To see
a circus
clown
with a
painted
face;
one face,
happy.
One face,
sad.
He gave me
his
blanket.
I thanked
him
before
he got on
his
bike
and
rode
away
into
the sky
wearing only
a tiny
red ribbon
bikini.
I wrapped

the blanket
around me
so as
to hold
my
body
tight.
I stood
upright
looking
at the
tilted
moon.

Buttered Dreams

These be my buttered dreams   imagery
of my heart impressions and soul repressions
revealed   delicately
as the wings of a butterfly
come to be at my side, intentionally,
meaning to rest on my arm,
but I'm not pleased, or at ease – brushing it away.

Many times I try to injure the butterfly,
to murder the butterfly,
but it cannot be dispirited nor displaced,
for it is a reflection of my internal face.
Now, resting on my arm for me to see
as dreams in pictures on my naked sleeve
in silent touch of me.

No more thoughts that kill   bash the butterfly
with a fighting fist. But wait! Be still. *See, feel*
the most beautiful butterfly is in life, at rest.
An illusion in colours sparkle as one with me.
And, from this, I may come to what conclusion?
Still, bewildered at my act – having been so utterly
deluded, detached, delirious, devious – unkind.

Now, to find, magic has been my saviour, as before,
seeking hues of hope in fading seconds.
Almost debilitating myself. Thinking the butterfly
was a festering blister pulsating on my arm.
Pus   poking at it through sorrows that blind my eyes,

needles up and down her spine.
Taunted by these sensations in my grief,

only to be saved from a final blow to my mind.
Concussed   then, seeing with settling visions.
Love has wings of a shimmering kind:
purple, blue and green. Fluid and smooth
as melted gold that gleams. Liquid sun
shine of day. Radiant and at play.
As in love   the butterfly in dream,

fluttering, muttering dreams.
Aware I have been dreaming – vivid dreams
so real – they seem. I was the sky wide.
My heart, the burning sun. Eyes shined
stars of night. My breath whistled as the wind.
And now, to be stirred from my sleeping.
Are these dreams for my safekeeping?

Like memories that fade; forgotten or altered by time,
as all that lives must surely die,
even the pictures inside my mind
like prayers that end   flowers bend in the heat.
Yet, to rise again. Knees stiff and sore and a back bent.
Bones of chalk in a body turned and twisted
like toes, blistered, by hard leather shoes.

SESTRA

Upon her heels, peeled skin, cracked toes,
overgrown nails, yellow soles – a pair.

Dirt, malted leaves, bark, seed; spare me the details.
Elegant hands, fingers on screens, chase, charm, talk.

She talks, I hear and see her   across the room.
Ancient looms, ancient wisdom in books,

ancient paths entwine the two of us.
Flesh, fresh, pink and red,   soft sponge.

Ancient woman with veiled eyes, velvet skin,
beneath the ancient sun – rises and falls.

Travels along the shadows, down market lanes,
by raucous sounds – bargaining for a carpet weave.

Magic coins and magic sands, lanterns, coloured jewellery,
Pipes – smoke rising through the holes of a crafted lute.

Almond eyes, dark circles, ponds – children and mother
are waiting for father to make his way,   into her day.

Kisses the stars; kisses her sunburnt shoulder, her nape.
Her womb ripe, fig-like   sprouts.

Crystal ball promises more.
Crossed legs   by the temple,   she begs.

Reads from a closed book of golden verses
and silver full stops – and skies to live for.

Presses her pen into her side and cries.
Vines drop from the roof of her house.

Flowers bloom,   cat meows—
away   from the polished floor,

a money plant grows towards   the ceiling.
Pots, pans, empty clamps, ancient cushions.

Takes the hem of her pants and folds them over,
folds them over, folds them over into a   pyramid.

Down the Nile   she steps   on fertile land.
Smiles and laughs, smiles and laughs, runs and runs,

turns and dances by herself and laughs – joy, oh raven joy,
iced drinks on a freezing day. Red balloons, white ribbons,

concrete outdoors and soldiers at war—
tears,   and the dying call.

They call her and she answers them.
They love her in their dying breath.

She roams over corpses, upon her heels and peeled skin
and cracked souls, overgrown stories, life tales,

repeating in spirals, full moons, shells, whispers—

coiled inside her bleeding womb.

Starlet moments, painted tissue, kissing – *flying hair*.
Love – malted woman – stark – seed.

Spare her   the interlude.
Ceremony and celebration and dedication.

More than words or gazes or foreign places or palaces—
silver and gold. Open the coloured faces, open them all,

to her elegant hands, fingers on screens, chase and talk.
Kisses upon her eyes and velvet lips, and ancient depths.

Into her house, and there, flowers bloom, cat's meow,
purr, feeling for her, ancient words.

Piano keys and a green clock waits for every second—
brooms and bed knobs, satin robe, naked breasts.

Starving people eating sawdust and each other in the dark.
Hooded women and men in the dark, quiver, quarrel, *kill*.

Turns her back to begin a solitary waltz – Chopin,
diamonds in ears   sparkle.

Pushing trolleys down aisles – bran, honey, soy—
stop!

Chocolate and nicer things—
white socks,   three pairs,   ancient shoes,

heels, skin, toes, nails, soles,
details.

The Word

1
In the beginning there was the word:
the word was light,
the light was truth,
and the truth screamed out in pain.

Mother,
give up your child to the wind.
Sing, mother!
Sing!

Father, finally you have come.
How lovely you appear before your opposing star.
Your brute fists—
she smooths with evening cream, and scented leaves.

She moistens your fired cheeks, weary-hearted.
She wraps your chest around her arms.
You are tired—
the night is late.

The day is long.
The life is short.
Who keeps score upon the battered shore?
Dunes disappear by her eager stroke.

It is no wonder – birds have wings and fly away.
You have feet and arms and die.
The song clicks on   and on   and   on.

It softens the muted silence of his muted love.

She longs   and she longs.
She changes halfway through every half-lidded phrase.
She begins to dance – the darkness is beside itself;
it cannot believe its fortune.

2
In the beginning there was the word:
the word was light,
the light was truth,
the truth screamed out in hope.

Mother, I give you up to the wind!
I have grown – the earth is about to shake and scatter.
The one that was great will be lesser – the smaller,
will not appear as inconsequential as it did before.

Mother, I want more and *not* my father,
or the frenzied clapping
as a wild bear mauls my back…
hope again!

Believe in the possibility.
Seven years apart and passion.
You cannot imagine
how wonderful my life will be.

My resilience spawns a wanted child:
light eyes and rainbow skin,
no tongue   a crystal smile

and wings.

Upon falling sand and scathing winds,
I birth the world from my spoiled bowls – taunted bosom.
A heroine collects the fem from my scattered pieces, and,
I hope – I believe it can be something else.

3
In the beginning there was the word:
the word was light,
the light was truth,
the truth screamed out in joy.

Oh, finally!
Oh, finally!
What joy is this?
It is the greatest joy I know.

He does not mention my name.
He sees me, and braids my hair,
turns it into a bun,
wraps it in his overgrown love.

He is moved by the sight of me.
He thinks of himself a God, I, the sky.
The river runs, the spring – oh, joy!
Oh, long-awaited joy!

I smile happily – no pride,
no prejudice,
no fornication.

We are the flower before the vow.

Tremendous hoping mother, asleep in your grave,
poppies grow down hillsides,
people stop to speak to you and yet,
I answer their discontent.

Father was a non-believer in himself.
Then, his son sprang. His son sang a lullaby.
And all is well. *Oh, joy – all is well.*
Pockets full of tickets and greeting cards,

a gift wrapped in coloured paper.
Long weekends. Long nights and days.
The years are better and better.
There is no apprehension in me.

4
In the beginning was the end:
at the end came light,
the light was truth,
the truth was the beginning again.

Cats and kittens; baskets full of apples,
sunshine through an open door,
enchantments of this deliberate day,
and silence.

He feels me, and holds me.
I do not forget him.
All talk ends,

all dying ceases.

Dogs do not bark,
birds sit on the grass,
the ocean stills.
My most wonderful life.
(My most wonderful, wonderful life.)

Pregnant mother, I watch you.
You lean your head against a wall.
You speak to me—
for a time you waited

on street corners,
rattling your empty pockets,
pulling at your plastic stockings
and luminous nails.

I found a baby in your coffee cup.
Take sugar   in no time.
Rich sediment on your lips.
You gag.

I encourage you to taste the bitter mud.
Baby birds were taken by the mother cat
to feed her kittens   take sugar.
There is no wind at all.

TEMPTRESS

Temptress views the world with an eye fired red.
Sacred fem, tempting tales from minds of vulgar men,
dancing the silken sea-lines, toes on golden sands.
Lie down those dirty rods, which stroke thy dirty hands.

A princely man sits with noon at the hem of my skirt.
Does he know desire as feasting eyes approach?
Flirting flames burn his lips, as woman steals a *kiss*—
in my gaze, a song to his name, though, I sing alone.

Aisles of fallen lovers, upon which soiled feet sweep.
Gypsy men, their mouths molest the day with politics.
Catch a fleeting smile, as birdman waltzes on the moon,
and the swoon of gothics feature, so other, yet, in tune.

A hundred questioning tongues licking decaying sentences,
yearning for a love of life that waits on time for death.
Ice-cold teeth chatter glass words in lemon water delights.
Laughter smokes on ends as fingers flick at cigarette sticks.

INCLINE

Beauty to the day that
brought forth your eyes
from the wild.
Rejoiced at your birth,
solitude and stillness
upon the end of my lips.
Jewelled hair tasselled, tamed.
A question arose: *Is it he?*
Up, in the sky, I praise
and hope, in heart
for the yearning to not begin.
Gaze at my shoulder
at the joyous start
I have just begun.
Clench myself by twigs that
stick in dry summer's bed.
Bends his fingers
around my waist
to hold me, transfixed
by the splendid sight of him.
Once again this man
in step is quick to ignite
my passionate humming.
A woman, he inspires.
I go to remove my shoes
to sit. Wanting to shake
my ripe and tender hips.
For his pleasure *only*.
Desire passes a feather

along my arm – soft skin,
tickles and shivers.
Turns my thought, instead.
Touches – I wish.
To extend my hand to his.
I move to the tips
of the edge.
To admire
a fragment of treasure.
Bury in my sigh
the fragrant of my bloom,
my seed awaiting.

Autumn Leaves

Noises of people walking by.
Drunk joys ravage the solemn,
but they are not solemn;
they close another chapter,

crooked
and craving
what the moment
has stolen.

I watch them with my senses,
alerted to my incredible scope of perception.
What lay beyond the end?
Another end. Another end.

Do you recall happiness a while ago?
Cups of lolly tea.
Spearmint and musk,
a must for any child to know.

I am a woman:
my lips talk,
my eyes see.
My heart is woven by silken thread

through the souls of men.
A babe and the autumn leaves.
On wet days I step a distant parkland.
What do I find?

Joys of solitude at the end, my friend.
You are my friend;
you simply appear
then disappear.

Breathe

Rest the canvas in the window;
it's weary from standing all day and night.
Put the brushes in a bottle,
leave the bottle by the door,
if you please.

Watch you don't step on the colours
and mark the polished floor.
The oils are over there,
on a scrap of waxed cardboard.

Ah, yes, so it be:
turpentine has spilt upon the floor.
Dab it with a page of crumpled paper
from yesterday's news.
It makes your nose burn, does it?

But, I tell you,
I've certainly come to like the smell.
It doesn't bother me anymore
to breathe.

End of August Nights

Where is the love we celebrate, where has she gone?
This is the life by which Demeter was born:

mystics and misters, madams and Adams.
Eve at eleven, poets and pilgrims.
Pan – players of pipes and fanciful flutes.

I cannot see her, mother, three cheers
and she suddenly appears. I see her—

dancing on the porch, like a torch
in the wind, and shining.

The Muses sing a happy birthday chime.
I too, amused, and somewhat out of tune.

A daughter is coming and she will be prized of thrones,
rare treasures, travelling camels, and exotic caravans.

She will be weaned on tales of heroes and heroines,
adventures of Kings and Queens—
bequeathed a divine kingdom – of no illusion.

Friends of Demeter will bring her half of Virgo,
in their bloodied hands:

grand pleasures, desert tents, harems,
dreamt of magic sands, and scents.
They love her so, and this she knows.

Whisper Seconds to Minutes and Hours
stand close to hear the promises of Time.
Oracles churning by the shrine.

Hermes breaks a bottle upon the floor
and outpours burning desire,
to ignite a trail of vamps on fire.

Seize my trembling hands young man,
before another bottle breaks upon the floor.
The frail one dreams to be all that she is not.

Passion – passion – I swear to you
nothing less than my total compassion.

Hesperus of west, let out your wistful sigh.
Diana, Diana, oh, lovely Diana, it is Eros – it is I.

Aurora wipes her eyes;
she does not mean to spill her tears from a paper cup,
to fill a wishing well with her rancid luck.

She hears her name and turns to see a reflection, clear.
From beneath a veil the silhouetted lips of night
are entwined with lilac threads.

Hope is a crust of silver souls risen upon a heart of gold.
She, in spite of Nyx and her darkened eyes,
in Ouranos' infinite sky.

Words of wine are rarely untrue, but of sentiments
running a distant shore, and wanting for more

amid the revelry of Gods in contest and Echo—
her prophetic telling.

The Sirens, maidens' wondrous songs and ancient gongs.
Lest I forget, as Memory in winter's dying breath, begs.

I will not be shocked by a bellowing cry
when spring throws her seed to wind.

OLIVE TREE

By the olive tree, on a perfect afternoon,
the night before is a pleasant memory:
sips and spilt port—
art in brilliant colours.
You led me to a field—
a white horse appeared,
as if from my dream, many dreams ago
and yet, it was from life,
more real than life.
The olive tree with its bitter fruit; I think:
My mother ought to prepare a feast;
bring sweetness to our table.
A pause – extends a hand to your heart.

You speak of a place secret to me,
you allure me like no other,
your spirit allures me like no other.
Made of sunlight—
transforms my mediocrity
into something unforgettable.
Pregnant in me with hope,
opening in me a door
never before turned on its hinges.
I prostrate myself upon the ground,
releasing every mistrust
for a moment of fame and glory,
in my life story.

I hope again – then think not to hope.
I have it all in me.
Whether you come or go; perhaps
we shall never meet again, as promised.
Our interest may wither,
as does the solid earth.
Soil the air with dust, and remnant times.
Subdued anticipation—
the dreamer has only ever the dream.
'Tis the adventurer who lives as I dream to live.
Might there be an adventurer in the woman—
I am brave. Rest my hand on your shoulder
as the olive tree bears witness to my advance.

Summer's Eve

The sky cries out; it sheds its joy for you and me
beneath its darkened moon.
For the heart knows when,

knows when to die, and birth again,
when to fly stars asleep in a black ocean swell,
where woman made of water cries, she sings,

she cries, aloud, and sighs.
Scribes my dreams on paper screens across the shadows.
Might he see into my secret starry eyes?

There, a fire burns the end of every night, and my soul
assumes the colour of an ancient light, and flickers,
before the one who comes to me of man,

with love to touch my hands along his pleasure,
wet lips to fill windy empty spaces
on the faces of a raining summer's eve.

Queen of Dance

He was dance and so he danced.
People, all people from all worlds
watched the dance,
wishing they too were dance.
Dance soared and scooped the ground,
was still   and moved,
was still in movement and *vigorous* in silence.
I came to watch dance dressed as man,
enthralled and yearning for myself.
To know a body that feels uninhibited—
undefined,   exhilarated
because it can, and it can,   and it can
take all of life and still pose as man,
a wild individual with electric hair.
Dance wrapped in translucent skins,
breathed in the wind—
drums sounded his step,
paving a way through the park
into the minds of people – some
afraid of themselves.
And so, I watched dance,
reluctant to dance, yet
yearning to dance as he;
the queen of dance was he.

After Dusk

Nyx, let down your raven hair upon moving waters,
anticipating Dawn's precision; without delay
upholds a prominent symbol, with every turn.
A rounded fullness brooding in your stomach;
breasts, in need of extraction by a gentle hand.

Mother, take hope, if you please,
forgive us our trespasses—

as we rampage through your drawers,
searching for secret content—
dreams and the wandering stars,
though, you hold to no possessions,
desperate for renewal and radiant bloom.

You are of our weary time;
might we ask for your wise counsel?

You say:

*"Darkness nurtures, wind whistles,
the knowing looms – in thieving shoes.
The babe who crawls upon the eleventh hour
rises, then hobbles, like a crescent moon.
Falls into night's sky, dies – at the horizon,
sleeps eternally on the rippled sand
by the shore – of my frothing kisses."*

VENUS

I see into a pool, her face is a mirror.
Venus sits by me and smiles.
She goes forward and cups her hands,
drinks from my spoils.
I watch her drink all my tears dry.
Venus is more beautiful than spring,
and woman is the promise she brings.

Venus brings me a book: the answer to why.
I open it to look inside and *butterflies* *fly*
like children who think not to dream
but do so as easily they breathe.
She offers me a jewel from her hands
into my eager hold, an emerald stone;
the size of all my wants.

From the dirt I dug and spat upon,
my toes, grows a garden
of every flower ever loved
and beauty to adorn every heart.
Flowering in every soul is a wealth of gold.
Venus gives me one flower to keep that
will never die. Says she: "Love is why."

Demeter

Who is she, teacher and mother to-be?
That one so radiant a beam as hope in trouble.
I am her daughter—
before a dream as daughter, I will be born once more.

> *Mother of fields*
> *and forests*
> *and orchids*
> *and spring.*

Wets her tears, not in sadness at winter's barren lands,
thorny stems, and broken sticks,
but in joy of shooting seeds in starring eyes
buried below the surface of soles of feet.

Ground torn, bruised skin – beaten.
Morning dew greets the wanderer about to be reborn
into her sweet and eager mothering arms.
She folds and wraps her chick.

Who is this woman of age ripe?
To give extra life, and flesh, and breath.
She waits patiently as decay burns from sun.
Scolds and flames and sees ahead of the fire next time.

She has drowned in floods that destroy her creations
of a splendid life. Still, she lives and goes along with me
on her familiar path,   she knows—
mother is patient as love ought to be.

She cannot be bought by sunlight and colours,
and thundering shows – ice on snows.
Or pleasure other than her own child, she knows—
I aspire to be reaped of she, this the primal urge in me.

Enchanted

If the sky be God's perfect blue, then
heaven I have found deep within you.
Life reflects her beauty in thee—
glorious stranger, who endears his spirit to me.

Your blessed self has captured my heart
in a glance that sees not its own passion.
My slumbering self has awoken to see
a flower of Eden grown especially for me.

Linger within my theatrical mind, modest actor,
until I call for the curtain to fall.
Pronounce your lines in quiet splendour.
An audience awaits with bated breath.

Forget you not my companion in mind
with those ageless eyes in an infinite stare.
My written words will keep these memories of mine.
In hope, our paths will cross in time.

Such enchantment is born of country morns.
Eyes that love without touch of skin,
sing a song – yet utter not a sound,
smile a dream without restful sleep.

Beautiful one, who speaks in silence and moves in stillness,
artisans painted a thousand words beneath your brow.
Seldom does one see pictures as revealing as these.
I imagine they were pictures painted for me.

3.
RISEN

ANCESTORS

Let the ancestors come,
let them rub red ochre up my sides
into the pits of my arms.
Over my legs, the red earth gleams.
Brush me all over with dust—
an elder speaks and I know:
immeasurable joy is at hand, at foot.
Upon the splintered light,
circles in every space.
Spider's web,
ringed tree,
sun in my eyes.

ROMP

World will *wobble*.
It turns around and around and around it goes.
Oh, the merry-go-round.

Still, still, still I sit, silent I sat and stare.
I see and saw with eyes as round as saucers.

Teaspoons, teacups, teabags on sugar cubes.
Tart, tea-tart, tongue on tart   tea   tart   tongue.
Squeal, squeal, the kettle does squeal, steam, and sweat.

Rain rains   hold the reins when the rain is raining,
racing racehorses round the racecourses,
radio (rain) man reports on races.

Mad, mad, glad to be mad, mad to be bad, mad in mind,
meticulous, mischievous, mysterious.
Me, my   my maddening mind   me oh my.

Glad to have met you, Madam.

Spot the frock   woman in frock.
Hat, gloves and frock   trot-trot   trot-trot.
Flamboyant, fluorescent frock – *how fantastic!*

What a frock!

Knock-knock at the door,
unbolt the lock.

Enters woman and frock.

"Oh Sir," she says.
"See she to my seat"
smiles she, seductively.

"Oh, yes, please," Sir says and shines his sheen at she
as he shows sensual she to her splendid seat.

Here he comes, come, come, came, cum on his pants.
Pant, pant, pant.
He comes to pause on his pant.

"Excuse me dear, nature calls – has come to call collect.
I shall call again.
Come back for more."

He goes   he went,

she rises to open the vent.

I AM EVE

God made the world in six days.
And woman, she came from a rib of man.
So, today, here I stand with a hand full of sand
and a mind as clear as a summer's sky.

Tell me, what am I to do with a hand full of sand?
Build a castle with a moat all around?
Then, I will order the trumpeters to play as I stride
as I think, how I will conquer the man in the moon.

Tell me, how am I to conquer this man who assumes
that my glances in the night are a fixture on he?
If I reach for the sky, I pull apples from trees,
but the Lord did not make me with wings to fly.

So, I close my eyes – pull the curtains tight,
for the battle I foster is played out of sight
and I splendour at the peace of my lonely life
as I dance in my skin to nature's delight.

I am woman, I am woman, a woman again.
I am woman, I am woman, a woman again.
Hear me clapping my hands to joys of my womb.
See the moat of my castle as a bleeding wound.

Adam is running from the river red.
The doves are flying on this lovely day.
It is life I bring forth and not his end.
I birth our kind, again, and again.

Onto the seventh day – a woman's rest.
She opens her eyes to confront her demise,
but the man in the moon is suddenly shy,
for he looks towards me and covers his eyes.

Why is the man in the moon so surprised?
Can he see my form in the light of tonight?
"I am Eve, I am Eve." I call out to he.
"I am Eve, I am Eve." I call out to he.

All I can hear
is his quivering breath
as I stretch out my arms
in a naked address.

Madame Fire

Men of clay, of dust turned and toiled,
come forth ye to ravage the vamp.
The seductress, she has awakened.
She, of raven passions and delights.
Her legs are smooth and plum,
her love consumes the man,
he dreams to know her.

Wanderer and rebel of spirit,
tears the earth with her teeth.
Tongue – bruised and battered.
Benevolent heroine,
she rises the sun.
She, of Gods created.
To the heathens, she runs.

Scattered poppies in her eyes,
scattered dreams in her golden skies.
Rejoices her own return.
Into the fields to die for, she lies.
Into his burrow, she rests her head,
crowning him by her glory—
her magic revives him.

Pleasures of the underworld.
He moves her into oceans of rapture.
She sins. Woman; she, of breasts
to please – to ask for – to give for.
Jewelled and tender – inspires in me

a desire for her empire.
Madame of kings is born of *fire*.

Beloved

Hear my cry—
I am dying and rising again.
My beloved, this day,
we share from our dreams;
you are no longer a dream in my sleep.

This time, here, is of no tomorrow
but of tears sour and sweet,
as the wines of kings and peasants, akin,
poured into our cup overflowing—
desired by all.

May I shout into your ear?
So you can hear me honour you.
That I may hear me too:
"I am alive. I am born again.
I am that which is one, this is me."

Having denied that which I am for so long
and now to laugh into a song of joy.
I am saved from death as I lay there dying,
in thought of a death that loves no one,
of the joyless and the depraved.

Yes, it be—
I lived as the dead once dying
before you saw as my eyes.
I walked in the shade of broken suns,
before your breath touched my skin.

Asleep in my waking hours,
I dreamt of you—
before I knew your name.
Dumb, though I had a tongue that turned,
I hummed a tune before you sung it again.

I tell you, I was all this, and more,
before you moved in me.
But no more, my beloved—
I have risen.
I am as the sun, loving.

Dug out with your hands
from beneath the ground.
To stand again, as before—
as in lifetimes before.
Though, I had forgotten,

as do stars in night and day shine,
but are not always seen.
In love, as was the first love
and the last love,
which has been and is yet to come.

Fear

I hear fear as it sings a solemn tune, and near.
I am unmoved.

I feel it rubbing its tongue along the earth.
Before I step, my toes are wet,

scratching its fingers down my neck.
Fear has come to win me back

as lovers do of a tragic affair;
they go together and come apart.

How very much fear hates tomorrow
and today, only in love with yesterday,

preferring the company of delusion,
suspicious of its own elaborate illusion.

Fear is a reliable mate,
always waiting at the gate

to welcome me into a darkened abode.
Once, and for so long a time,

I knew fear not by name,
understood not the rules of game.

But something has changed:
in and out of me,

fear comes around; and again,
embracing the air I breathe.

But something has *surely* changed.
I am unmoved.

I am not afraid.
But, here comes fear again,

holding out its chain.
Something has changed.

Fear begs and grasps my hands *desperately*,
obscures my sight

with remnants of sentimentality:
"Remember, when we were such good friends

and we spent all our time together?
Let it be, as we were then."

I am unafraid.
I am changed.

Fear builds a cage to hold me in,
but fear cannot win because I love.

Love is unafraid
and I am *changed*.

Matilda Bay

Fill me with words to paint a picture,
serene, to honour such a perfection.
Though my brushes lay at rest,
my fingers numb are ever eager
as I come to reflect upon a morning
graced by an end to May,
naked is my virgin soul, though
dressed by feathered wings of day.

Oh me, oh my, where be
the hidden world on this day?
That I find myself alone in calling
for nature's encore by the bay.
How does one begin to explain
to absent friends and foes?
A performance bestowed upon me
by the will of heaven's throne.

Splendid sky, caressed by your breath
within which captured beginning's rest.
Though chilled to the core of self,
I do not step aside,
for one begs for this moment
to linger in my heart forever.
If time be not one's enemy,
I would not hesitate in thought.

A splash of divinity is sightly
for my sleeping eyes,
woken to these startling subtleties

of yet another life. Lights—
of a thousand life-dreamt fantasises
entice my mind. Thus, questions
the silence: "Who restores me
to this long forgotten scene?"

Trolls liaise wickedly with shadows
beneath wooden legs.
Broken shells and tortured tongues
scatter along the river's edge.
Foolish fellows gather together
beyond the play of nature's way.
And, so one moves to shed a tear,
knowing for this dying day.

Song

Children play
beneath summer's tree.
The wind b l o w s ,
moves the world about
their hair,
is hot upon their brows
to the east.
The sun stands into noon.
The afternoon assumes
its descent.
Childish dreams
cooled by night,
starry flights,
and dancing shoes.
Costumes
sparkle
moonlit folds
embraced
by a shawl
of pure pleasure.
Merely, child's play,
entirely dreamful.
Flickers of eyes
taken from the sky
soon
will
turn
towards
day.

Breeze

In stillness, time does steal a breath
as silence wades above one's head.
Feel the wisdom at your crown
when a sigh heaves beneath the ground.

Dig a hole in the sky
whilst the flesh waits to die,
then a truth may be told
to all the young and all the old.

Lick the breeze upon your lips,
touch it with your fingertips.
Hear it walking on the floor
as it hurries through the door.

See it not, but know it true:
the living spirit comes from you.
Thus, slumber not upon this earth
whilst another babe mourns its birth.

Trust the day to know a liar,
spoken words do fuel the fire.
Close your eyes to shade the light,
hold your tongue throughout the night.

As you linger in the dark,
embrace the visions of your heart.
And as you move amongst the trees,
know yourself to be the breeze.

WISE, OLD

On tip-toes, children reach for the sky.
Another year on and they jump for the sky.
The older one gets, the more they do try
with dreams in trees and a will to fly.

Now, I am old, I talk to the cat
with words at my ears, licking my hat.
I am alone and I sigh to that,
knowing my wisdom rests at the mat.

Tomorrow my legs they move with the breeze.
With the tops of my shoulders brushing the leaves.
Though, there is no one I care to please,
I slick my brows to honour the trees.

Next week, I stroll with the clouds at the beach,
throwing to sea the seed of a peach.
Nodding at gulls that stand out of reach,
I listen to lessons that mermaids teach.

The day then comes for me to die.
My eyes, they shut to bid goodbye.
My silent breath dispels a lie
for children with their arms stretched high.

On the hill, the strangers meet
whilst noon, she walks in retreat.
Here, I come to take my seat
in the sky beneath their feet.

Green Grasses

I am standing in a field of green grasses:
green grasses to my north, south, east, west.
The hills are green like the grasses.
Oh, green grasses all around me!
I see not beyond the green of my eyes.

Green of the warmest kind welcoming me.
Green of the coolest day,
refreshing my lungs with scents of love and life
and a love for life which cannot be described.
Here, I stand, oh radiance, splendid vision,

you embrace me with your kindness.
I am alone. Alone, I am. In bliss and serenity.
My heart throbs, pulsating with rhythms of self.
My breath sounds, increasing in tempo, velocity, passion,
oh, I cannot contain my joy. I will rupture, I must run!

I run as ribbons run green, tongues licking at my knees.
Silken tongues tickling my fancies as fantasies erupt,
captured in the beauty above. My hair flutters in the wind,
sings to the open sky as open as my heart be,
as blue as the soul's sea, crystal clear as God inside.

I soar! I soar! My arms glide at my sides,
the wind pushs against me in playful caress.
I soar. I sigh. Fill my lungs, oh breath of life,
fill me with lightness, as magic descends.
A child's joy sounds:

a joy unnamed, untamed, unknown.
But to the green fields, this is no stranger.
Endless, everlasting, the child is mine, within.
Can I run and stop to dance, and laugh?
With the ribbons of love, my friends.

Let us play all day, roll and prance and lay.
I lay on life, and look upon life.
I am surrounded by life – *oh, I am life!*
Life – you revitalise me and ripen me
so that I stand amongst the grasses so green

and fly with the breeze—
and there's the sun…
the grasses whisper secrets in my ears,
blazing secrets of kites and ribbon streamers in flight.
Thus, I ascend to the sky, I fly so far and wide,   so high.

I see the grasses each by each, I see them all.
I know them two, four, six… rejoice! It's feeding time.
I join the herd   *I sway,*   I sway back and forth.
See my face draped in golden lace, suckling the teat of life.
Mother – mother sun – see me too.

"Oh child, I see only you."
How splendid! The taste of milk is sweet.
I hold out my hand for mother's reach; *I want more.*
"Hide not your face beneath the shadows – call
and I will come to you with honey nipples."

I climb   I climb   the highest hike.

The mountain's peak within my sight.
How strong I feel, so strong and straight, and loved.
I shine, radiant me, beautiful ribbon of love.
My face touches the warm bosom of life.

Electric   eccentric energy   gathering you to me.
Carried on the back of wind, an angel messenger of love:
"Take more of me, my love, take all of me, my love,
so that you may grow closer, and then, we will be one."
Oh mother, I strive – but day will end.

"Worry not of night's subtleties for father will descend
to widen your vision. Strengthen your stride.
Again, I shall appear with morning's delight!"
With silence, she sleeps. In silence, I sleep—
amidst the awakenings of night.

OH, LIFE!

Pleasure!   *Oh, pleasure.*
Breathe life deep into your lungs.
Feel your body move in and out – *in and out*.
Seek the pleasures of day and night.
Know no limit,   let   limit   die.
Reach forth for the sky, night or day.
Seek the colours before your eyes.
Climb the clouds, you need not wings to *fly*.
Open your mind and imagine the unimaginable.
Do not refrain from speaking your truth.
Rip out your tongues and glue them to the sun!
And then you may speak of glory, of vision–
to know the story of the universe.
You cannot see from your seat on the earth.
Know more than the ground you sprout forth from.
Seize   this   m o m e n t   of   life—
life, in all its wonder, move in its mystery.
Do not hide your face beneath the sheet.
Do not dream beneath the sheet.
The sheet will draw the breath of life, of love,
of total splendour from   you.
Eject your arms and legs, and lie them by the bed.
Escape whilst you still can from the shallow, the subtle,
and leap into the depths of water.
Your toes are at the shore of pleasure.
Leap forth—   be not afraid.
The doom you live in fear of, resides with you.
Doom is no stranger;
you have welcomed doom through your door.
Undress it. Reveal it. Dismantle displeasure.

And you will know what it is, to live.
Shun not from life, *delight in life!*

What Dreams May Come

Water flows…
we build a float of dreams and sit upon the float,
and f l o a t   downstream.   Into a valley
we arrive and post our flags and chant our creeds—
by an altar of peculiar perceptions.
We drown the fools and swim in pools,
so c o o l   upon our skin.
We see in the sky, with one eye—
secrets hanging by threads. Secrets live and secrets die.
We lie on our backs with our heads drowned.
From a popular scene, a clown wants his blanket back.
Well, how about that!
I cup my hands and drink of the holy water.
I'm a fish, in a dish of good times, in love with everybody.
How fine the sand does shine beneath my fingernails.
I'm a bubble that b u b b l e s and *burps*
on the edge of a line, in a moment of no time.
I'm fine. Feeling so f i n e .
I dive into the divine and dance in dazzling palaces
across   alien   lands.
Ride on crystal balls over worlds colliding.
Dive into a mirror dialogue where jewels talk with minds
a d r i f t .   Melt into a retrospective.
I'm dealt a pack of pasts; a ghost from my memory
shakes me out of my adolescent fumbling.
I love with a velvet glove.
The kindest thoughts, I pick and choose:
Mould my tongue with honeydew.

WEDDED VOW

Model of man and woman perfectly formed.
Golden man and golden woman. In love.

We are of love. The wedded vow is love.
The golden seed is the golden flower.

Vacant streets bellowing with bursting bulbs.
Vigorous possibilities, unlimited destinations,

e n d l e s s   days and nights.
Stars in our entwining hair, browse and burrow.

Companions invigorate each other in festivity,
    frenzy.

Great fortune inscribed in coffee cups, saucers,
            aroma.

Spectacular conclusions ignite new beginnings.
Forget not from where now comes.

Recall the feeling of the moment,
intensely lived, intensely vibrant.

So much so, that the outline of description pulsates,
friends pulsate, folk pulsate, the newly spawned pulsate.

Heaven and earth rumble and rave, and the golden room
hums.

The scene moves – my fantasy moves and grows.
He celebrates a turn at every corner.

Love ruptures, love wails, love allures.
Love thrusts the senses against a furious satisfaction;

p u l l   s
and
dis
man
tles
all expectation.

For this love, that has no depth, or shallow,
is extreme in its extravagance.

Knows not a wall or halt and, yet,
contemplation begs for an understanding of love.

Love so impossible, love knows not itself.
Love so complete, love knows not itself.

This, is the love to which we aspire, not to know,
inspired by love, to love forever more.

So, do the spaces know not from where they come,
the trickle longs to flow out suddenly, and copiously.

It is dawn that breaks the morning with birdsong—
and only ever at dawn.

Morning calls around the world at every second.
Love is said to sound from this continual fervent song.

Golden Eyes

Tremendous joy,
rampant feasting upon rapture.
Drinking of grace from golden cups:
elegance, charm, full gazes.
Impregnated imaginings:
colour, laughter and beauty.

Above all else,
beauty encrusted, encapsulated,
withheld from withering winds.
Short of tomorrow. Now! Now! Now!
Only ever now. Tomorrow now.
Yesterday now. All time has come to now.

Waiting for now has been some journey
as heels have tread the ground.
Inside shoes. Soft skin, toes hindered.
Toes wanting a freedom from shoes.

Golden shoes. And golden eyes.
Love. Love, soft. Love, hindered
and moulded. And wanting flight.
Golden love. In golden eyes.

Intimacy

I have been fondled by the Gods.
He has a fire beneath him
over which he walks the burning coals.
To touch my thoughts, in reach.
I, in reach across an illuminated sky
know of myself in him.
He is the caress of the wind,
brushing at my fired cheeks.
The clouds, our parting sorrow.
The sun, a promise birthing the morrow.
It is now a closeness.
It is now the struggle and resolution as one.
It is now that we live together.
My knowing is in the unsaid.
His binding love, in the silence of his breath.
In spaces transpires an exchange
of intimacy – given, then taken.

ONE LAST TIME

I like the sky,
you like the clouds.

I like the moon,
you like the stars.

I drink tea,
you drink coffee.

At an empty street café we sit.
Favour me with grand thoughts. I smile.

"Life and death, one last time," you say.
"All dreams grow old and spoil."

Like my words, for real – my friend.
Like my heart, of sounds and sin – again.

The girl becomes a woman today.
Did you say? Did you see her?

Did you like to play?
"Be real, I am the music."

In mind, he reaches for my eyes and stars
entwine our steps to dance for and clouds

rain upon the virgin and wet her soul, she frowns.
Yes, favour me grand friend. I smile.

"For my life," you say, and still,
only the table is real.

To Love

1
Have you the night?
I give night to whoever passes me.
Take the moon from my eyes—

have every dream I have ever dreamt alone,
and tears, and calls into the solemn.
I am favoured.

I may do without praise or promise.
For, I am the one who feels glorious.
I am the one who has love.

To love with an open wound that itches
and salt, and I do not wince.
Take the night – I give it to you.

Not another thought, enough!
Not another imperfection or quarrelling night
or rampant day   unfulfilled worth.

To love her locks of hair smelling of sweetness.
Takes the feeling of every bloom into my hand.
A bunch of black roses resume the light.

Her cascading sentiment hinders my voice.
Let me be silent,   still.
Let her voice speak.

Take the night out of my heart,
and ash will
fall.

Tame my stoop and the night will be gone forever
from my memory,
to love you *desperately*—

to hold you in the folds of my transcendent hope
revolting all existing shadow,
to hold you; to deny you a pending conclusion.

To deny a feast; the thirst and hunger of a famished lot
who boast fullness without her,
to deny the beggar every ease in a possible death,

and yet, by all compassion,
to surpass that which was once of life so grotesque,
to leap from the scene appearing so familiar,

and taunted, and teasing,
tempting every sorrow.
Love, I am at peace with my mortality,

that withering recessive self.
Pricks feathers into open pores
and climbs a tall height.

Drunk by intense labours.
Pours forth the brewer's potent pleasure;
fired pleasure.

Up in air—
I take flight,
unhesitant in love's company.

2
Night, you have lost me and not to day.
Not to life. Not until the end.
To love, in one single sight

between her propelling, rounded and eager breasts.
To endure allure of almost impossible proportions.
She is the cause of all her fame.

Take courage in this moment,
and then, willingly proceed
to consider her bloodied lips,

bloodied by kisses that pu ll and   run.
Wet as oceans in charging motions—
to always come and go as she pleases:

to miss her embrace and my sunken face,
inverted by the surges inside myself.
To endure hardship in her recline;

to rejoice her return upon shores as deep,
as long they roam.
To love, as I have loved,

I cannot describe nor enact a play on any tragic stage.
No audience will I please with scriptwriter poise

nor would they ever believe me,

in my youth and inexperience.
I, having never had a lover to hold in my arms—
I have love.

I, having never touched the dream in my reach—
I have love.
I, who has admired the shallow night

and adored the distant horizon.
I have bathed in the sight of hands on shoulders,
never mine – *I have love.*

Passion, love, and love for passion:
to love,
to that which I was born.

To love, as others fear to be without her,
as only few could love.
To love, I give my final breath and every breath.

Walk upon the earth, and raise my will to heaven.
Reduce my intelligent consideration—
postpone my interrogation.

Release my beating heart and pulsation.
Praise the mud, navel and crown of jewels.
Oust moral inscription from public view.

To love, I move in words—

to lift you to your feet so to see her
and cradle you – to feel her ideal texture,

to know her untamed beauty.
Her purpose without meaning
and meaning no purpose…

I fail me yet, to unclothe her waist to her plum flesh,
to define her innate and enduring attraction,
to recall her rich wisdom in any language—

every description
is short
of her.

Being

Letting go of a promise once made
to someone or something;
whispered to—
as I lay sprawled and examined
looking at the stars – my drunken gaze
altered by numerous travels
to the same place,
but a different way each time.
Drunk not on wine or fermented spirits,
or the sight of my arms
falling—
to the side of the world
as I *spin*
like a ticket to nowhere.
But here
I have arrived somewhere,
and for all that has gone,
one has come.
For all, that will not be met by me,
I will meet with many yet
as I have met with one.
By every shadow, the sun stands.
By every storm, calm steps in time.
I have not been waiting
forever.
I have been waiting
always
to know the silence
in myself.

Rebirth

Beyond the stars on a starry night,
my eyes seek a distant sight.

Whilst I'm seated on my throne,
a story rises from my throat.

Hear this tale as it comes to you,
knowing it could be true.

Stretch your arm into the east
and you will come to dress in west.

Dip your tongue into the north,
your mouth will come to speak of south.

I did lay myself down to sleep with stillness at my reach—
I slumbered the wilds of the deep
when upon me dawned the voice of a silent sparrow,
woken in the early hour by the presence of eternal power.

The unknown at my feet, I burrowed beneath the sheet
Darkness at my head, I felt a weighing on the bed.
In that moment I began to pray for meaning,
thinking I may be dreaming, thus I wished myself away.

Courage in the belly – my knees turned to jelly.
My eyes swept fear aside and raced along the sheet
to meet the one who intruded. He. She. It. Eluded
my sensory vision, but not my primal intuition

for my bed still tilted as if pressed by lead.
Instead – my eye caught the flicker,
the flight of eternal light, though I heard some snicker.
Unhesitant, I revealed the deal.

These eyes lay sight on the most inviting holy light,
which moved with the clocks of the world.
It did twirl around and around like a top—
Bop! Bop! P o p ! Like the world.

A black dot in the middle, at the core of the ripple.
The lure of perfect love like a kite in flight.
Soothing my brow, hand at my crown,
fingers of a velvet glove, in love, how kindly.

And finally, some tension worth my time to mention.
In this revision, I will tell of my heart's division.
From the light there emerged a tormented spirit.
A man out of flesh amidst our sphere, yet lying so near.

I did not run away or hide—
I neither wished for him to stay.
I searched his blazed eyes to find a well of despair
more than I could bear. His lids rolled dry in sockets.

I could weep solemn tears for man with a peeled soul,
but I gasp at the sight of light,
the cycle of life that still dances in delight
before my raw remembering eyes.

At the post of my feet,

at this moment of our meet,
on the hour of an early morn,
again, I was born.

YALLINGUP

I was told I had come to a place of love.
Had I not met with her golden hair on this day,
I would have felt her, anyway—
for, in the sky her eyes, they stare at me.
And, as I walk, she follows me from behind.
I know her as I count the sands, how deep she stands.
As I retreat from her tears so sweet,
I know her kiss has touched my lips, salt-sweet.
In the coast – another side to her tortured smile.
If it were not for her elegance and majesty,
I would be overcome by her raw mystery.
And, though she holds me in her breath,
I find myself alone with words—
for, she speaks to me without a tongue.
Thus, I dream to know her thoughts.
As her brow sweeps her eyes goodbye,
I know that love is in my eyes.

AUGUSTA

By the direction of a friend,
I found a beginning and an end.
There I stood with the sky, ocean and earth,
not knowing if I was upright, upside down
or lying on my back—
certainly, no in-betweens,
even I was something – not someone.
And with the breeze, I felt my heartbeat.
In the sun, I saw the moon.
One. One place. One life.
Just one and nothing more, nothing less.
I was neither master nor servant.
And people speak of heaven like it is a dream,
but I know I have not been dreaming this time.
I have found a heaven on this earth.
There is no divide:
heaven and earth be the same,
so too, night and day.
I have journeyed this life in search of self,
in search of truth.
Only to find, I am joined to you.
The world rests inside of me,
life and death are one.
No we. No they. No that.
And, so, I squat on the balls of my feet
with orange in the sky reflecting in my eyes,
but I have come to see orange turn to blue.
The ocean is the sea,
I am all of these,

they are something of me—
I know time stands still in myself.

Homecoming

God smiles at the blood
trickling from my toes.
Eager – as the sunrise,
rugged rocks,
sprays of ocean.

Colours of a carnival
at the edge of the world
where I stand with angels,
beauty awakens—
welcoming me home.

Sun

My golden steps   toes
glitter in powder of pollens
of things that grow and die.
Oh,   how they do nothing
but turn their heads
to see me come
and stare at me.
They sing:
"The sun has come!"

LINDA V. CULL was born in Perth, Western Australia, and into a traditional Southern European culture traumatised by war. At age fourteen, Linda was diagnosed with a disfiguring spinal condition which caused her pain and despair. Her recovery from depression and intergenerational grief began spectacularly at the age of sixteen when a series of transcendent experiences set her free.

Visit the author online at **lindacull.com**

www.ingramcontent.com/pod-product-compliance
Lightning Source LLC
Chambersburg PA
CBHW020424010526
44118CB00010B/409